j975.7
P223s

W9-DGF-529

1/2019

WI

States

SOUTH CAROLINA

by Bridget Parker

CAPSTONE PRESS
a capstone imprint

Next Page Books are published by Capstone Press,
1710 Roe Crest Drive, North Mankato, Minnesota 56003
www.mycapstone.com

Library of Congress Cataloging-in-Publication Data
Cataloging-in-publication information is on file with the Library of
Congress.
ISBN 978-1-5157-0428-7 (library binding)
ISBN 978-1-5157-0487-4 (paperback)
ISBN 978-1-5157-0539-0 (ebook PDF)

Editorial Credits
Jaclyn Jaycox, editor; Kazuko Collins and Katy LaVigne, designers;
Morgan Walters, media researcher; Tori Abraham, production specialist

Photo Credits
Capstone Press: Angi Gahler, map 4, 7; Corbis: Bettmann, top 18,
Gordon Parks, middle 18; Newscom: CHRIS KEANE/REUTERS, 15,
David J. Griffin/Icon SMI 953/David J. Griffin/Icon SMI, 29, Denis Alix,
middle 19, RANDALL HILL/REUTERS, top 24; North Wind Picture
Archives, 12, 25, 26; One Mile Up, Inc., flag, seal 23; Shutterstock:
Action Sports Photography, 10, Andrew Brunk, bottom 24, atanasija1,
bottom left 21, Bonnie Taylor Barry, bottom left 20, ClimberJAK, 6,
Cvandyke, 17, Dave Allen Photography, Cover, bottom left 8, bottom
right 8, David Brian Williamson, bottom right 21, Denton Rumsey,
14, DFree, bottom 19, Everett Historical, 27, forestpath, top left 20,
Fredlyfish4, top right 20, Helga Esteb, bottom 18, Jan Miko, 7, John
Wollwerth, 11, 16, Joseph Sohm, 13, Patricia Chumillas, top left 21,
Robert D. Howell, 28, Ryan M. Bolton, middle left 21, s_bukley, top 19,
Sean Pavone, 5, 9, Tom Reichner, middle right 21, Valentyn Volkov, top
right 21, Yongcharoen_kittiyaporn, bottom right 20

All design elements by Shutterstock

Printed and bound in China.
0316/CA21600187
012016   009436F16

TABLE OF CONTENTS

Want to take your research further? Ask your librarian if your school subscribes to PebbleGo Next. If so, when you see this helpful symbol 🖱 throughout the book, log onto www.pebblegonext.com for bonus downloads and information.

LOCATION

South Carolina is a small southeastern state. The Atlantic Ocean lies on the state's eastern border. North Carolina lies to the north. To the south and west is Georgia. The city of Columbia sits in the center of the state. It is both South Carolina's capital and largest city. The coastal cities of Charleston and North Charleston are the state's next largest cities.

PebbleGo Next Bonus!
To print and label your own map, go to www.pebblegonext.com and search keywords:

SC MAP

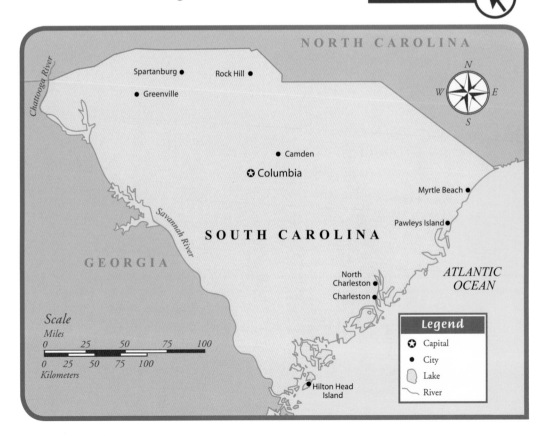

NORTH CAROLINA

Chattooga River

Spartanburg ●   Rock Hill ●

● Greenville

N
W   E
S

● Camden

✪ Columbia

Myrtle Beach ●

Savannah River

SOUTH CAROLINA

Pawleys Island ●

GEORGIA

North Charleston ●

Charleston ●

ATLANTIC OCEAN

Scale
Miles
0   25   50   75   100

0   25   50   75   100
Kilometers

Hilton Head Island ●

Legend
✪ Capital
● City
◌ Lake
～ River

Named after Christopher Columbus, Columbia is home to more than 133,000 people.

GEOGRAPHY

South Carolina stretches from the ocean to the Blue Ridge Mountains. Part of the Appalachian Mountains, the Blue Ridge Mountains stand in the state's northwestern corner. Sassafras Mountain is the state's highest point. It reaches 3,560 feet (1,085 meters) above sea level.

South Carolina's rivers flow from west to east toward the Atlantic Ocean. The Santee River, the Great Pee Dee, the Congaree, and the Savannah River are the state's largest rivers.

The largest lakes in South Carolina are not very old. Dams created Lake Murray, Lake Marion, and Lake Moultrie in the 1930s and 1940s.

PebbleGo Next Bonus! To watch a video about historic Charleston, go to www.pebblegonext.com and search keywords:

SC VIDEO

Folly Beach Pier in Charleston was built in 1995 and extends 1,045 feet (319 m) into the ocean.

The Congaree River floodplains make up Congaree National Park, ideal for swamp-growing cypress trees.

Legend

▲ Highest Point

⬮ Lake

⛰ Mountain Range

〰 River

Scale

Miles

0   25   50   75   100

0   25   50   75   100

Kilometers

Sassafras Mountain

Chattooga River

BLUE RIDGE MOUNTAINS

PIEDMONT PLATEAU

SANDHILLS

Lake Murray

Congaree River

Savannah River

COASTAL PLAIN

Lake Marion

Great Pee Dee River

Santee River

Lake Moultrie

COASTAL ZONE

ATLANTIC OCEAN

N W E S

WEATHER

South Carolina's climate is warm and wet. July temperatures average about 90 degrees Fahrenheit (32 degrees Celsius). South Carolina's winters are short and mild. January temperatures average 50 to 60°F (10 to 16°C).

Average High and Low Temperatures (Columbia, SC)

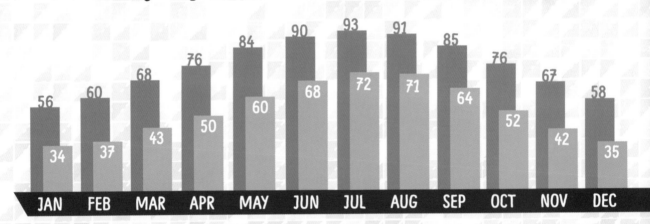

	JAN	FEB	MAR	APR	MAY	JUN	JUL	AUG	SEP	OCT	NOV	DEC
High	56	60	68	76	84	90	93	91	85	76	67	58
Low	34	37	43	50	60	68	72	71	64	52	42	35

LANDMARKS

Myrtle Beach

Millions of people visit this coastal city each year. It has beautiful beaches, shops, restaurants, hotels, and entertainment.

Darlington Raceway

Nicknamed the track "too tough to tame" and the "Lady in Black," Darlington Raceway is a NASCAR favorite. Its unique egg shape creates interesting races for drivers and fans.

Fort Sumter

The American Civil War started at Fort Sumter in the Charleston Harbor. Today visitors can ride a ferry to the island fort and see the historic cannons used in the war.

HISTORY AND GOVERNMENT

Major Ferguson and his men are defeated by Colonel William Campbell at the Battle of King's Mountain in 1780.

While native people have lived in South Carolina for thousands of years, French and Spanish explorers arrived in the 1500s. Settlers faced starvation, disease, and wars with native people. They had trouble keeping settlements going. In 1670 people from England settled Carolina Colony near Charleston. In 1710 the colony spilt into North Carolina and South Carolina. During the Revolutionary War (1775–1783), American colonies won their freedom from Great Britain. South Carolina became the 8th U.S. state in 1788.

The government of South Carolina has three branches. The governor is the head of South Carolina's executive branch. The legislative branch of South Carolina makes laws. It is called the General Assembly. There are 124 members in the House of Representatives and 46 members in the Senate. Judges and their courts make up the judicial branch of government. The judicial branch decides whether someone has broken a law.

South Carolina's capitol was originally in Charleston before moving to Columbia in 1790.

INDUSTRY

South Carolina is a leading manufacturing state. Carmaker BMW and airplane-maker Boeing are two large employers in the state. South Carolina also makes other goods such as chemicals, rubber, plastics, machine parts, and textiles.

South Carolina is a top lumber producer. The state grows large harvesting forests. Farmers also grow tobacco, cotton, soybeans, corn, and wheat. South Carolina is one of the country's largest producers of peaches.

The state's natural resources, such as the ocean coastline, also make tourism and fishing a big part of the economy.

Together, the areas of Charleston and Mount Pleasant create the state's leading fishing port.

The BMW plant, a large automobile factory, is located in Spartanburg.

POPULATION

   Most of South Carolina's population is white with European backgrounds. African-Americans make up the next biggest ethnic group in the state. More than 1 million African-Americans live in South Carolina. This includes the Gullah people who live in the low country islands. South Carolina's population also includes small numbers of other ethnic groups such as Asian, Hispanic, and American Indian. The Pee Dee Indian Tribe is one of the American Indian groups still active in the state.

Population by Ethnicity

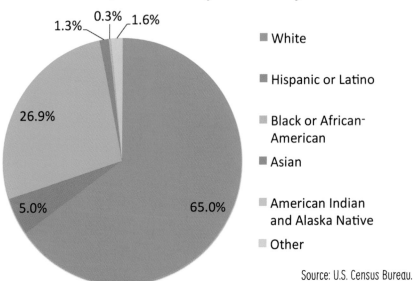

1.3%   0.3%   1.6%

26.9%

5.0%

65.0%

- White
- Hispanic or Latino
- Black or African-American
- Asian
- American Indian and Alaska Native
- Other

Source: U.S. Census Bureau.

Gemstone

amethyst

Fruit

peach

Amphibian

spotted salamander

Animal

white-tailed deer

Music

the spiritual

Dog

boykin spaniel

FAST FACTS

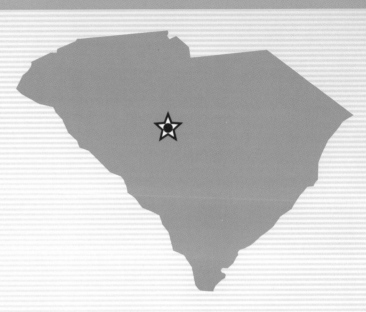

STATEHOOD

1788

CAPITAL ☆

Columbia

LARGEST CITY •

Columbia

SIZE

30,061 square miles (77,858 square kilometers)
land area (2010 U.S. Census Bureau)

POPULATION

4,774,839 (2013 U.S. Census estimate)

STATE NICKNAME

Palmetto State

STATE MOTTO

"Animis Opibusque Parati," which is Latin for "Prepared in mind
and resources," and "Dum Spiro Spero," which is Latin for "While
I Breathe, I Hope"

STATE SEAL

The state seal shows two scenes. On the left is a palmetto over a dead oak tree. This represents South Carolina's defense against the British in the Battle of Sullivan's Island. South Carolina's fort was built of palmetto logs. The British ships were oak. Around this scene is the state motto that means "Prepared in Mind and Resources." On the right is a woman who stands for hope. She walks along a beach full of swords. This represents hope overcoming danger. Around this scene is the motto that means "While I Breathe, I Hope."

PebbleGo Next Bonus! To print and color your own flag, go to www.pebblegonext.com and search keywords:

SC FLAG

STATE FLAG

On South Carolina's flag, a white crescent moon and palmetto tree are on a dark blue background. The palmetto tree honors the June 28, 1776, colonists' victory on Sullivan's Island during the American Revolutionary War. The fort the colonists defended there was made of palmetto logs. The blue background and the crescent moon are from the flag that flew at Fort Moultrie in 1776. This flag was used as a signal to British ships that colonists were in charge of the fort.

MINING PRODUCTS

portland cement, granite, sand and gravel, limestone

MANUFACTURED GOODS

chemicals, plastics and rubber products, machinery, motor vehicles, airplanes, and vehicle parts

FARM PRODUCTS

greenhouse products, cotton, peaches, tobacco, soybeans

PebbleGo Next Bonus!
To learn the lyrics to
the state song, go to
www.pebblegonext.com
and search keywords:
SC SONG

SOUTH CAROLINA TIMELINE

1500s French and Spanish explorers arrive in South Carolina but have trouble maintaining settlements.

1620 The Pilgrims establish a colony in the New World in present-day Massachusetts.

1670 English settlers begin Carolina Colony near Charleston.

1710   Carolina Colony splits into North and South Carolina.

1775–1783   South Carolina helps fight for independence from Great Britain during the Revolutionary War.

1788   On May 23 South Carolina becomes the 8th state.

1860   On December 20 South Carolina becomes the first state to leave the Union and form the Confederacy.

1861–1865 The Union and the Confederacy fight the Civil War. South Carolina fights with the Confederacy and suffers heavy losses of property and lives.

1914–1918 World War I is fought; the United States enters the war in 1917.

1930s The Civilian Conservation Corps plants trees and improves parks in South Carolina. This provides work during the Great Depression (1929–1939).

1939–1945 World War II is fought; the United States enters the war in 1941.

1963 African-American and white students begin attending public schools together.

1989 Hurricane Hugo hits South Carolina in September.

2002 U.S. Senator Strom Thurmond from South Carolina celebrates his 100th birthday on December 5. He is the only U.S. senator to serve at age 100.

2009 North Charleston gets a Boeing airplane manufacturing plant and assembly site. This helps South Carolina recover from high unemployment during the Great Recession (December 2007–June 2009).

2010 Nikki Haley wins election to become the first female governor of South Carolina.

2015 Dylann Roof opens fire in Charleston Church, killing nine people, including the church's pastor and a state senator.

Glossary

activist *(AK-tiv-ist)*—person who works for social or political change

census *(SEN-suhss)*—an official count of all the people living in a country or district

ethnic *(ETH-nik)*—related to a group of people and their culture

executive *(ig-ZE-kyuh-tiv)*—the branch of government that makes sure laws are followed

ferry *(FAYR-ee)*—a boat or ship that regularly carries people across a stretch of water

industry *(IN-duh-stree)*—a business which produces a product or provides a service

judicial *(joo-DISH-uhl)*—to do with the branch of government that explains and interprets the laws

legislature *(LEJ-iss-lay-chur)*—a group of elected officials who have the power to make or change laws for a country or state

starvation *(star-VAY-shuhn)*—the condition of suffering or dying from lack of food

textile *(TEK-stile)*—a fabric or cloth that has been woven or knitted

unique *(yoo-NEEK)*—one of a kind

Read More

Felix, Rebecca. *What's Great About South Carolina?* Our Great States. Minneapolis: Lerner Publications Company, 2015.

Ganeri, Anita. *United States of America: A Benjamin Blog and His Inquisitive Dog Guide.* Country Guides. Chicago: Heinemann Raintree, 2015.

Hess, Debra. *South Carolina.* It's My State! New York: Cavendish Square Publishing, 2016.

Internet Sites

FactHound offers a safe, fun way to find Internet sites related to this book. All of the sites on FactHound have been researched by our staff.

Here's all you do:

Visit *www.facthound.com*

Type in this code: 9781515704287

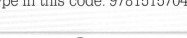

Check out projects, games and lots more at
www.capstonekids.com

Critical Thinking Using the Common Core

1. Which three lakes were created by dams in the 1930s and 1940s? (Key Ideas and Details)

2. What two nicknames are given to the Darlington Raceway? (Key Ideas and Details)

3. Look at the pie chart on page 16. What percentage of South Carolina's population is Black or African-American? (Craft and Structure)

Index